Helps for the Separated and Divorced

Learning to Trust Again

Reverend Medard Laz

LIGUORI
PUBLICATIONS

One Liguori Drive
Liguori, Missouri 63057
(314) 464-2500

Imprimi Potest:
John F. Dowd, C.SS.R.
Provincial, St. Louis Province
Redemptorist Fathers

Imprimatur:
+ John N. Wurm, Ph.D., S.T.D.
Vicar General, Archdiocese of St. Louis

Censor Deputatus:
Robert G. Ditch, M.S.W.

Contents

Introduction

"I grew up thinking that divorce only happened in Hollywood. Now it's happening to me."

How frequently such words are spoken today. Divorce touches the lives of so many people — spouses, children, sisters, brothers, grandparents, and friends. Divorce is a modern-day epidemic. One out of every five people in our country is presently separated or divorced, once was separated or divorced, or has come from a home disrupted by separation or divorce.

This booklet does not try to solve the problem of divorce or even to explain it. Rather, it attempts to deal with the central issues that people face as they go through a separation or a divorce. If you happen to be one of these, it will provide support in your suffering, as you face the loss of your spouse. You are not isolated in what you are feeling. You are intimately involved in one of life's greatest mysteries, that of death and resurrection. Everything material and human can die. And, because you are human, it is possible for a marriage to die. This does not mean that the two of you were utter failures. You may well have given your all. But for some reason your marriage has not survived. The important point is that *you* need to be resurrected, that you find new life.

Death and resurrection are basic to life. As with your spiritual life, the emphasis must be on resurrection. Once you have experienced your loss and wrestled with your grief you may be tempted to withdraw from all social contacts. But this is not real living.

This booklet will help you to *go through the pain* of your loss and find resurrection or new life. You, of course, want to run from the pain and avoid the grief of your situation. Newspaper ads and TV commercials constantly urge you to put on your happy, "I'm OK" mask. But often you are miserable and anything but OK. So why fake it? Why bury your feelings or avoid expressing them? Going through the stages of your grief rather than steering clear of the agony will eventually lead you to a new beginning in life. This rebirth is worth the price of your pain.

The Beginning Experience weekend, founded by Sister Josephine Stewart, S.S.M.N., in 1973, will serve as the basis for the topics dealt with in these pages. Encountering yourself, working through the grief and the guilt, trusting again, deepening your relationship with God, and closing the door gently on your marriage are key issues in starting over again in your life.

These subjects are presented on the Beginning Experience weekend by a team of persons who have faced separation or divorce in their own lives. There is time for reflection and writing and also small group sharing in order to promote an inner healing for the twenty or thirty people who are in attendance.

Sister Josephine Stewart deserves profound thanks for her tireless efforts in nurturing the Beginning Experience throughout the United States and other countries of the world. Many thousands of people like yourself, who have lost a spouse through divorce or death, have received a healing touch by Sister Josephine Stewart and the many team members who minister to the brokenhearted. Thousands of people owe her a debt of gratitude.

Medard Laz

1
Not a Failure

"My whole world caved in. I put my whole self into my marriage and it died. All of my hopes and dreams are over. I feel like a failure. Why should I want to go on living?"

As you survey the wreckage of your marriage, you find it almost impossible to see things in their proper perspective. Everything is hazy and cloudy. Your marriage is dead. You, too, are dying. No matter the cause or the circumstance, your innocence or culpability, you surely feel like a failure. Marriage is supposed to be forever — in good times and in bad, in sickness and in health. Your marriage has now become a nightmare. What formerly gave you pleasure — couples holding hands, words of love songs, courtesies you see other couples sharing — now give you pain. Emotionally, you are as raw as a piece of meat on a butcher's counter.

At some point you will have to sort out the difference between the failure of your marriage and your own personal sense of failure. The two are very distinct. Engrossed in the problems surrounding your divorce, you cannot see the distinction. But it is there and it is real. Your marriage may have failed for many reasons. But this does not mean that you personally are a failure. The marriage may well have been doomed from the first date or soon thereafter. Immaturity, lack of conviction, financial woes, addiction to alcohol, extramarital affairs by your spouse, or parental interferences may have brought your marriage to its knees.

You may have given far more than the proverbial 100 percent in trying to make your marriage work. The fact that it did not work is no shame to you.

Looking back, you can more clearly view some of the things that went wrong. The blame you place on yourself makes you feel guilty. This is normal. Yet, most of the time, you did your best, or what you thought was best *at the time*. Today you may regard the past in a different light. Back then there was no way that you could. You have grown from that past. You are now in touch with the milestones in your history. You must not make them your millstones. Cheer up, you have survived a most difficult experience — the death of a marriage.

As you seek to discover your new self, there are four things you must do: (1) learn to control your emotions; (2) sort out your life; (3) make a personal inventory; and (4) watch your relationships with others. These areas need to be *worked through* and not passed over. This is exhausting, painful, and often lonely; yet the end result is an integral and loving person.

Learn to Control Your Emotions

You are on an emotional roller coaster. You experience many highs and lows as the inevitable happens. Emotions that were on an even keel are now unbalanced.

"I can't live with my spouse, and I can't live without him."

"I'm so relieved to be alone, yet I feel abandoned."

"I finally feel tranquil inside, but the world around me is driving me crazy."

"I had to get out of the house, because I feel like I'm drowning in an ocean of pain and doubt."

Your emotions will rarely flatten out at this time in your life. As with a roller coaster, all you can do is hang on. Express your feelings as best you can. Sit with a friend. Talk with a clergyman or counselor. Attend a self-help support group. The roller coaster will eventually stop or at least slow down, but be prepared to travel on your own timetable.

Sort Out Your Life

Most people find it rather difficult to physically and emotionally sort out their lives. Although this is not easy, it is important. Separation and divorce throw your whole life up into the air. As the various parts land, they need to be gathered up and sorted out. Where do children, money, job, parents, in-laws, friends, personal belongings, relaxation, social life, etc. fit into your new life-style?

Your natural inclination is to resist this sorting, this redefining of priorities, because you have many doubts or qualms about the separation and the divorce. Yet, if you are to become the good and loving person you are inside, you need to do the sorting out. You look at old family portraits, and tears fill your eyes. It is hard to find the energy to get your new apartment settled and looking homey. Yet you have God-given inner strength to help you make it.

Make a Personal Inventory

After you have sorted things out you will see the need for a personal inventory. In your entire life you may well have never taken such an in-depth look at yourself. You were always someone else's child, spouse, or parent. You never had to ask, "Who am I?" Directions were always given to you. "Do your homework." "The car needs fixing." "The garage needs cleaning." You were raised to fit the role. There was always another job to do, another role to play. Now there is no given role for you to play or mold for you to fill. You detest your jobs and your new roles. It is time for self-evaluation. Many questions should be asked and answered. Here are but a few:

- What are my strong points? my weak points?
- What do I like about myself?
- What makes me happy? sad?
- What do I especially have to give to other people?
- What values do I hold dear to me? Am I willing to part with any of them?

9

- What kind of person am I right now?
- Am I a giving or a selfish person?
- Am I an optimistic or a pessimistic person?
- What do I plan to do with the rest of my life?
- How relaxed or playful am I?
- Can I easily laugh at myself?
- How do I rate myself physically? spiritually? sexually?
- Do I say warm, loving things to others?
- How comfortable am I when in close physical contact with others?
- Why will I or won't I become close to a member of the opposite sex?
- What gives me the most satisfaction in life?
- How satisfying is my job?
- What are my goals in life?

It would be worthwhile to take the time to write out your answers to these questions, trying to express the underlying feelings behind them. Aware of your changing, often roller coaster emotions, try these questions again in several months and see how you have changed!

Watch Your Relationships

Going through a separation or a divorce, you are prone to jump from your emotional roller coaster to close, personal relationships with others. You do this to avoid the suffering of sorting out or taking a personal inventory. "Somebody is better than nobody" is a tonic that people often use when they are lonely or depressed. Yet, time is needed to pull your personal life together before getting emotionally close to others. A personal healing needs to take place.

You need someone who will listen to you and get you through the rough spots. But you do not need someone who will divert your attention from where you really are with your life. Any sorting out and taking of personal inventory is a task that belongs to you alone. Otherwise, you are merely using the other person in the worst sense of the word. If you give the impression that you are seeking a romantic interlude and then walk away, you are being very unfair.

It is essential to know who you are and where you are going with your new life before you can consider further relationships. When do you know this? When you have *worked through* the abovementioned areas and have also *worked through* the grief stages found in chapter 3. This may well take several years; but it is worth the wait, no matter how long.

Leo Buscaglia, the author and lecturer, raises a key point about life when he speculates that the Lord on Judgment Day will not ask you how successful you were in your marriage or your job. Rather, the question he will ask is: "Have you become the person who you are?"

2
Losses and Gains

Psychologists have pointed out that the average person can sustain two or three personal losses in a single year and survive reasonably well. Yet, during and after your separation and divorce you are presented with fifteen or more losses that are quite devastating.

It is vital for you to recognize and understand the losses that you are experiencing, in order that eventually you might turn these losses into gains. Long after the divorce is final you will ask yourself: "What did I really lose? What did I gain through all of this?" Our lives and our emotions can be somewhat like the items on our income tax forms. We have our losses as well as our gains.

Losses

The following fifteen losses are some of the major ones that practically every separated and divorced person experiences, and you no doubt have had your share of them.

Identity. In marriage you (as a wife) saw yourself as half of a couple; you belonged to one particular person, and he belonged to you. Now that person is lost to you. For years (as a husband) your real day (or week, if you traveled) began with "coming home." Your identity as a husband began at 6:00 PM each night or each weekend. Now you are but a part of a nameless, faceless crowd. Just as a wife draws tremendous meaning and identity from her husband, so does a husband draw from his wife. Divorce creates an identity crisis for both of them.

"Who am I now that I am no longer an equal partner in marriage? What is there to look forward to in the evening, with no one 'coming home' or no one there to greet me?"

Role. In and through marriage you viewed yourself as half of a couple — a Mr. or a Mrs. — each playing your roles and attempting to be fulfilled in these roles. As a husband you probably enjoyed the roles of being the provider and the fixer. As a wife you may well have enjoyed being the homemaker and mother. But alimony, child support, visitation rights, holiday schedules, and seeking full or part-time employment destroys most of the roles you counted on in marriage. Such simple things as gardening, balancing the checkbook, and wiping the dishes may or may not have been enjoyed. Yet these were roles played out that gave a meaning to life.

"I miss puttering around the house . . . just doing little jobs here and there. It was a relaxing way of spending the weekends. Without that I'm not ready to face Monday morning again."

Status. The loss of whatever status you have attained through your marriage can be disconcerting. As a couple you had a certain reputation that you generally enjoyed. Now that is gone. You feel marked as a "marriage failure." Your loss of status may mean turning in your charge or credit cards (and not being able to get new ones). Or it may mean that you can no longer belong to certain clubs or organizations.

"If I'm no longer a 'Mrs.' then I am a 'Ms.'; but I'm too old to be a 'Ms.'; and 'Ms.' is like announcing to the whole world that I'm divorced."

"I have a hard time using the 'Mr.' anymore. 'Mr.' went with 'Mrs.' and there isn't a 'Mrs.' anymore, so why should there be a 'Mr.' anymore?"

Image. After your divorce you stand in front of a mirror to see what others see; and the self-encounter is devastating. You really notice the wrinkles on your forehead, the bags under your eyes, your thinning and graying hair, your splotchy skin, and the ever-present paunch around your midsection. The conclusion is frightening and you hate to put it into words.

"As a divorced person and the way I look — who'd ever want me?"

Spouse. Your spouse is your most obvious loss. He or she is simply no longer there. Your home or your apartment is now vacant in more ways than one. You sit down to eat alone (even if the children are present). Your wedding pictures (and all those other pictures of you two in happier moments) — these you are tempted to destroy. They are vivid reminders of what once was but will be no more. Even though you have been separated for some time you still feel the gnawing loss. Someone seems better than no one.

"So many years of myself, day and night, I invested in my spouse, and now my spouse is gone forever."

Horizons. When you are married or are part of a family, there are always new horizons ahead — having children, watching them grow up; enjoying holidays, vacations, birthdays, and anniversaries; changing jobs, moving to new places; going into retirement; starting new hobbies; and participating in endless family activities. Separation and divorce put a damper on all of these. What was or could be great joy for two people is now agony for one. You are afraid to face tomorrow. What is there really to look forward to?

"I lie awake in the morning. I shut the alarm off before it rings. I do not want to hear it. I don't want to get up and face today. There was nothing to look forward to yesterday. Why should today be any different?"

Sanity. You question your sanity when you recognize that you feel both hate and love for your former spouse. Perhaps you have muttered to yourself several times: "Am I losing my mind?" On the one hand there is still a deep-rooted love that you have for him or her. This goes back to the early years of your marriage, and it is not easy to erase — no matter what has

14

happened since. Yet, for all that you have endured and the hell you have been through, a deep-seated hate has also mush-roomed.

"I've never felt like this in my whole life. I'm not myself. I've never hated anyone in my life, and here I am hating the person that I married. And still I'm in love . . . am I going crazy?"

Children. If you have children, you experience their loss through separation and divorce. As the father, ordinarily you will see them only at the times the court decides. As a mother — even though you may have custody of the children — your contact with them will be less than before because of your work away from home and the time they spend with their father.

"My children seem almost like strangers to me. I'm with them a lot. But it's not the same. They're in their own world now after the divorce, just like I'm in my new world, I guess."

Parents, In-laws, and Family. Because of the divorce, that sense of failure (which you must strive to overcome) will also be felt by your parents and in-laws. In fact, they will feel betrayed. They have so much at stake — their own success as parents in raising you, regard for the family name, love for their grandchildren, enjoyment of holidays, weddings, and family events. All that they were looking forward to since the time when you were born, now seems to be ending in disgrace.

"The hardest thing was telling my folks that we were separated. I felt like I was killing them with my words. After I told them, I never wanted to see them again, I was so ashamed."

Friends. The loss of friends can be a brutal ordeal as your marriage ends. Lifelong friends may say: "Now call us day or night if we can be of any help." Then they seem to disappear from the face of the earth — no Christmas cards, hospital visits, or phone calls. Many of your married friends cannot or do not want to understand your new marital status. To some you are a threat. If your marriage failed, so can theirs. And they want nothing to do with any divorced person who might break up their own marriage. Most of your friends live in a "couple" world, and since you are now "unattached" you are considered "unfit" for the backyard barbecues and the New Year's Eve parties.

"I wish I had contracted cancer or leprosy instead of getting a divorce, the way my friends have abandoned me. I've made myself available for sports and social gatherings, but my friends are cool or make excuses. And the neighbor across the street who for over ten years has waved to me as I drove by now all of a sudden keeps his head bowed."

Job. For many men, separation and divorce will mean a change of jobs. At best, this is a lateral move. Support and familiar faces are gone when this happens.

For almost all women, separation and divorce will interfere with their homemaking tasks. You need a job to support yourself and your family. Or if you have been working away from the home, a new, better-paying job is required.

"I changed jobs, but I'm not satisfied. I have more responsibilities and have to travel more — for too few extra dollars. And that money goes back to the children a lot faster than I can make it."

"I enjoyed cooking and keeping a house — even watching soap operas. To keep myself going, every day I have to put up with a boss who is no older than my own son."

Money. The truth of the old adage, "Two can live as cheaply as one," becomes abundantly clear to those who have been divorced. Supporting two households, starting a new household, paying off the lawyers, and the cost of counseling service, additional phone calls, eating out, and babysitters — all these add up to a lower standard of living for both parties.

"My car is falling apart. I run to the bank with my paycheck to cover the checks I have already written. Going anywhere on vacation is out of the question."

Familiar Surroundings. As the husband, you felt "at home" after work and travel, even if there were monumental problems in the marriage. Everyone needs to feel "at home" somewhere, to belong, to have roots. After the trauma of divorce, finding a new place to live is most unnerving. Coming home after a day's work or on a Friday afternoon to unfamiliar surroundings may well be like exile to Siberia.

As the wife, you soon come to hate your home. Offering little enjoyment anymore, its maintenance becomes overwhelming. There is no longer another adult with whom to share your home. What was once your home is now your prison.

"Coming home in the early days of our marriage was such a joy. Now 'coming home' merely means going 'someplace.'"

"I turned the key, opened the door, and walked inside. I had this overpowering feeling that the house had died."

Church. Many separated and divorced persons cease going to church once the break is made. Pounding on heaven's door has not saved the marriage. You feel like a stranger in your own church. The homily is geared toward family life, and you feel singular among all the families sitting near you. You think of all the happy church celebrations — the Christmas carols, the Baptisms of your children, and the weddings.

"When I'm in church, I feel alone in a cavern, even though I am surrounded by other people. The memories should all be happy ones, but now they appear strangely sad."

Daily Rituals. During the years of your marriage, you have kept certain rituals; you slept on your side of the bed, had your turn at the bathroom, sat in a particular chair, gazed out the one window, and ambled to the refrigerator for a nighttime snack. Now all of that is disrupted. The pattern and the purpose of your life has changed. Your divorce has changed many of your daily rituals.

"I don't know where to turn next. I keep bumping into everything. I'm not sure where anything belongs, not even myself."

Gains

The abovementioned losses may seem overwhelming, but fortunately there are certain possible gains awaiting you after you have weathered the initial storms of your parting. These can eventually balance and even outweigh the losses that you have had. The gains that you will be reaping are the following.

Image. You can find the real *you* as a result of resolving your inner turmoil. This comes through the examination of your own weaknesses and strengths as you try to discover why your marriage failed. Admitting your weaknesses, as well as discovering that much of what happened was not your fault, carries a cleansing element into your life. It is possible that your former spouse put you down or made you feel worthless by implying that you could do nothing correctly.

"I'm happy with myself today. When I see something about myself that I don't like — my hairstyle or my corpulence or my irritability — I make a change and I'm a lot happier."

First Name. In today's world, your divorce will give you back your first name (and, if you are a woman, possibly your maiden name). As a child you may have been straddled with nicknames. Marriage took care of that, but now the marriage is gone. Now the emphasis is off your last name and off the "Mr. and Mrs." Being addressed in letters, memos, and phone calls by your first name gives you a new identity before the world. You are an "uncluttered" human being, without the nicknames or the formalities.

"When I received my first letter with nothing but my first and last name, I felt that I had become a person, responsible to no one except myself. This was a wonderful feeling."

Intangibles. What it took you years to acquire in your marriage — the house, savings accounts, and furnishings — will quickly be sold, divided, and dispersed. But certain intangibles that money could never buy will now be yours — receiving *your* first paycheck in years (if, as a wife, you were strictly a homemaker), being able to sleep until noon on weekends, staying out late, or not having to hurry home. What you have is now truly yours in the real sense of the word.

"Before, all I did was worry about dust or uncut grass. Now I'm seeing that so much of what we owned just meant a lot of worries. So the house needs painting. It will eventually get done."

Independence. In marriage much of your life was controlled by your spouse; as equal partners, you tried to please each other. A great deal of your emotional life was centered around the other person. Now the control of your life, your own destiny, has been handed back to you. *You* now make the choices. If you made most of the decisions in the marriage, at least now there is no one to blame you for the wrong ones. It takes a long time to sort out your life. Once you do, you'll be in control. You can do as you please on a given Sunday afternoon or you can put off supper until you are ready to eat.

"The air I'm breathing is so different. The final months of the marriage I thought I was in jail. Now that my divorce is final, I feel that I've been paroled and given my freedom."

Peace of Mind and Heart. This is no doubt your greatest gain after the divorce is finalized. Those sleepless nights and fearful days — the result of unbridled rage and excessive drinking — have now ended. Your first really good night's rest after it is all over is heavenly. Seeing a glimmer of a smile on your child's face means that life is returning to you and the family. Not having to worry about being used or abused is a great relief. Depression can initially settle in, but eventually an overwhelming sense of peace will come. "Peace be with you" was the gift that the risen Lord came to give you.

"Every night I'd worry about what time she'd be getting home, if at all. Now that all is final, I don't have to worry anymore. What a relief!"

A New Beginning. By nature you are a builder, like your Creator. People build in different ways: families, friendships, projects. Much of the building that you were doing in life got delayed as your marriage was grinding to a halt. Now you can get back to the opportunities that await you at work or with the family. You can return to school to finish some courses. Each day after your divorce you arise to less sorrow and more joy. There is healing; there is hope.

"Not long ago I'd wake up with a curse on my lips. 'Why hadn't I died during the night?' Now I can't wait to face another day. Even the problems are now challenges and opportunities. While married I had one life to lead. Now I find that I've been given a second life to live."

New Friends. Throughout the years of your marriage you probably limited your friendships. The ones you had were primarily with other couples. But the void in your life left by your divorce can be filled with new friends. The exciting aspect of your new friends is that *you* are choosing them. Formerly, they were — of necessity — your next door neighbors, business associates, room mothers from school, or acquaintances from church. Your new friends are ones that are attractive to *you* — because they care, they understand. You enjoy being with them, and your growth as an individual is often a result of their friendship.

"I lived so long thinking that my spouse could meet all my needs. My new friends help me to see life as ever so beautiful. I have great fun doing with them things I never thought of doing when I was married. How I enjoy an all day bike trip."

Quality Time with the Children. In going through the divorce, you thought of *Number One*, namely yourself. This was necessary for survival. Money, job, and the house also weighed heavily on your mind. Only then, perhaps, did you consider the children. But after these major issues are resolved, or at least settled in some fashion, the importance of the children can be reestablished. As a mother, your time with them can now be quality time. You can deal with them directly — talking, playing, or disciplining. You no longer have to worry about your actions so as not to offend your spouse. With the anger and the coldness gone from the house, a "new" family life can begin. And, as a father, your time with them on weekends and vacations away from the house can be very enjoyable sharing times.

"The children's questions are certainly deep. I never knew all of what they had in their heads. I don't always have great answers. Often they put me on the spot. But we are all growing. We are closer than we ever were before."

New Appreciation of Your Attractiveness. As your marriage died, you began to ask yourself: "Why look presentable?" What was the use in looking attractive if your spouse did not really appreciate you?

Now there is great excitement and fun in getting dressed up and going out. To discover that you are appealing to others is important. For too long you have either had no feelings or felt like a neuter. Slowly but surely you can once again enjoy being your attractive self — whether you are a man or a woman.

"The first time on the dance floor after my divorce I thought I was doing just great. After two dances my partner softly whispered to me to stop trembling. I hadn't noticed. Today I enjoy dancing with many partners. It has been a long time since anyone has told me that I trembled on the dance floor."

Security. In your marriage, down deep you were seeking security — financial, emotional, and occupational. As the dark clouds appeared, the rug of security was being pulled away. Would the bills get paid? When would your spouse be home? Would it be another day for a big fight?

Today you do not have a surplus of funds and there are many loose ends; but most of all, day by day you are becoming more secure. You may have to do it yourself, but the bills will get paid. You no longer need to wait up for your spouse. And the only fight you have to worry about is the one that you start.

"Before my divorce I was so tense that I needed tranquilizers. Now my heart is my home. No one can deprive me of my new home."

New Anchors. Many of the things listed above as losses — family surroundings, roles, friends, and daily rituals — were anchors that gave purpose and meaning to your life. Now these are gone. Slowly but surely, as your ship of life begins to steady itself amid the turbulent waters of divorce, you will be able to drop new anchors. You will become more comfortable in your apartment or home; great fun can be had with new friends. New roles of cooking and cleaning, painting and auto repair will give you much unexpected satisfaction. New daily rituals for reading time and preparing breakfast will make for a "new" you.

"I was so afraid of the downtown area. Now I enjoy taking in a play or a movie or going to one of the museums. I feel like Columbus discovering a whole new world."

Personal Vision. So much of your marriage was a couple affair. In marriage you were bound to another person. Rather than deciding what was best for you or your own personal goals, you were asked to consider what was best for the marriage and the family. This was as it should have been. Yet, this was limiting. It was easy to fall into roles and ruts and not always view life as a mature adult. Having been in and out of marriage, you should have a whole new understanding of what life is all about and what you have to offer to others. As you sort out your life, you pick up the pieces and fashion a new mosaic. There are pieces from yesterday, but they are fashioned by *you* into a new tomorrow.

"When we were first married how I enjoyed saying 'our' and 'we.' It's hard, but I am beginning again to enjoy saying 'I' and 'my.' I am starting to find a lot of personal satisfaction in this."

Integrity. Possessing the feeling that you did all that you could to make a go of the marriage is vital to you in your present state. You still have to be you, even after the marriage has ended. The courts can take away many of your possessions, yes, even the children. No one can take away your integrity.

As you stop reviewing the past and blaming yourself, you will find that you are very much alive and that you hold your life in your own two hands. Integrity arises from self-worth. You can now begin to set new values to your life.

"I felt so hurt and worthless during the separation. I felt drained of everything I ever was or am. Now I possess the greatest gift I'll ever receive — *myself!*"

A Deep-rooted Faith. This is no time in your life to depend on an immature kind of faith. You need a strong, deep-rooted faith that comes from a personal encounter with the Lord. And it will come to you when you talk to and listen to a Christ who has suffered and died. He will help you to better understand the way of your own Calvary. There are no frills to your faith life today. It is an adult faith, rooted in a belief in yourself — that you are going to make it — and in God who will help you to make it.

"Without God's help I wouldn't be here. I had absolutely no one to turn to during the day or late at night. So I talked to the Lord. Oh, how he heard me. He didn't take away my anguish. He gave me the strength I needed to endure my turmoil. I have found a friend for life."

New Challenges. At first you were laid very low by the weight of the many problems inherent in your new life. Now you have begun to turn these problems into new challenges. Soon you discover that you do have the ability to solve your problems. Encouraged by this, you will find great excitement and satisfaction in rising each day to uncover new paths to the heights you have set for yourself.

"I have shuddered every time I have seen mountain climbers on TV. 'Never me!' I have said. Yet, almost every day I climb my own mountains, grabbing onto the lifeline for dear life and pulling myself up higher."

3
Working Through Grief

Numerous writers have likened divorce to death; they compare the end of a marriage to the end of a life. And certainly the feelings surrounding both are similar — abandonment, confusion, loss, etc.

If your spouse were to die, there would be flowers and cards, church services, the comfort of a clergyman, as well as calls and visits from neighbors and friends. All of these expressions of concern and support would greatly ease your grief process.

After separation and divorce, however, spouses are usually left to solve their own problems. Divorce in our society still has a personal stigma attached to it. Children, parents, in-laws, relatives, neighbors, and co-workers often are not too supportive. They usually leave you and your grief unattended.

It is most important for you to recognize that the grief you feel so deeply is *normal* to life; it is as much a part of your life as eating or sleeping. Unresolved grief, however, can easily cause boredom, emptiness, coolness toward others, feelings of being in a rut, nerves, self-pity, sarcasm, and an overwhelming urge to escape at any cost.

As you journey through a separation and a divorce, you feel that you are the only one undergoing such a loss and groping through such torture. But so does the child whose helium balloon has just burst, the girl whose pigtails have been cut off, the teenage girl whose boyfriend has gone off to college, the expectant mother who has had a miscarriage, and the parents of a child who has just died. All of these suffer unique heartache at the losses they have sustained. Your grief is normal to your life process. Because you are so miserable, you feel that you are alone. And you *are* alone. The breakup of your marriage is your own personal loss.

Elisabeth Kübler-Ross in her book, *On Death and Dying*, speaks of five stages of grief that are present in the face of death: *denial, anger, bargaining, resignation,* and *acceptance*. These same stages of grief in confronting physical death are also present as you face the death of your marriage.

Denial

The first stage is that of *denial:* "No, this is not really happening to me." You do not believe that all of this trauma is occurring to you. Because of a great amount of personal shame, you say little or nothing to family members or friends. You make various excuses. "He's out of town on business," or "She couldn't come because she's not up to par lately."

You may well have been separated for months, yet you persist in denying it. Even when there is a third party involved you cling to the almost hopeless chance of reconciliation.

The initial desire to waive alimony can also be taken as an unwillingness to admit to yourself that the marriage has come to an end.

Extended denial of grief caused by a separation or a divorce can be extremely harmful. The denial becomes internalized and emotions are locked within. This hinders you from living. Your denial may at first seem easier — because you want to avoid the pain. But the longer you deny it, the heavier it gets.

Part of the denial problem stems from the fact that you cannot understand how a rather good marriage can end in divorce. You compare it with a fine book that you have read. The first thirty chapters or so are most enjoyable and make for great reading. But the ending is so deficient; it hardly befits the splendid, early chapters. You look on your marriage in much the same way. You and your spouse had many priceless and unequaled years together. But now your marriage has come to an unpleasant end. The last years of your marriage do not negate the good years that went before. And that is why you continue to deny the end of your marriage.

But when you refuse to close the door on the marriage, you bring yourself to a standstill. You have no zest for living because your marriage was not supposed to turn out like this. You grew up believing that divorce happened only in Hollywood. But not all stories and not all marriages have happy endings.

Anger

The second stage in the grief process is *anger:* "Why me?" you ask bitterly. The expression of anger by way of tears and tantrums is normal at such a time. But our society is so structured that it is difficult for you to voice your feelings. "Keep them inside . . . be brave; or, if you must, display them in the privacy of your own home." This is what society expects. But anger is present at this moment in your life, and it will not go away by itself.

Perhaps you have remained at the denial stage because you have been taught not to manifest your anger. "He still is a very fine man" (though he is living with his secretary). "She's a great gal" (though she has left her children and haunts the bars every night).

To display anger over the way life has gone awry is not abnormal; it can be a healing part of your journey through grief. If your anger is not allowed healthy expression, it may fix itself on the wrong parties — yourself, the children, your parents, or others.

This is not to say that anger should be exclusively and continually directed at your former spouse. Anger is better dealt with by sharing it with a counselor, clergyman, or friend.

Then an understanding of the anger can be acquired. Playing games with your ex-spouse — manipulating the children against him or her, castigating your former spouse every chance you have, delaying child support, not appearing for important family functions, showing up drunk for meetings, having blatant affairs — can easily mushroom into open warfare. These tactics can be most destructive, especially for the children.

The important consideration here is that you handle your anger in a *constructive* way. Rather than say "I'll show you," you should be willing to say: "I'll show myself . . . that I can face my losses as well as the many inconveniences of separate maintenance and still be very much alive."

It is essential that you search out people who, while understanding your anger, will check your excesses ("You're going to have to stop talking like that"). What you don't need is someone who placates you ("Don't worry; in six months you won't even remember what he/she looked like"). Let your anger dissolve into tears. Water makes everything else in the world grow. Surely your tears will also help you to grow.

Bargaining

Bargaining is the third stage in the grief process. Here all of the "If onlys" rise to the surface. "If only he'd stop his drinking." "If only we'd both agree to go to a counselor." "If only there weren't the financial pressures." "If only she'd stop going out with her girl friends." "If only his secretary wasn't in the picture." "If only the in-laws weren't around."

And then there are the "What ifs" about the past. "What if I had not been so naïve and our sex life had been better?" "What if we had not made that move?" "What if she had not gone back to school?" "What if we had not lost our child?" "What if we had not lived with our parents?" The list is endless. Yet at the bargaining stage, this is what you generally desire — a long list of bargains (page after page of them, like in the Sunday newspaper). But, like those Sunday ads, they are bargains that make life a bit cheaper but in no way free.

As you consider these "If onlys" and the "What ifs" you will notice that you are clinging largely to false hopes. You are waiting for a change of climate that in all likelihood will not come. Would you plan on a hot summer day in the middle of a Minnesota winter? This would be possible but not very probable. When you *and* your spouse look squarely at the "If onlys" and the "What ifs" and begin to work on them, then measurable progress can be made. When you *and* your spouse seek counseling, strive to improve your sex life, or struggle to reestablish your personal priorities, then a springtime is possible. Sadly, this is not often the case.

Prayer can be a part of the bargaining process: "If God will only bring my spouse back, I'll do . . . (anything)." Such prayers are worthwhile, yet they are often said in sheer desperation. You are hoping for a miracle. It is not that God is insensitive or that he wants such a misfortune to happen to you. God permits physical suffering and death in our world so that there might be a greater experience of life, either on earth or in heaven. In like manner, God may allow the death of your marriage so that you might be resurrected to an even greater life. Overindulgence in prayers of petition leaves little room for prayers of thanksgiving, praise, resignation, or forgiveness. Praying in this singular fashion might be your attempt to circumvent the hurt, the inner death and anguish with which you are struggling. If you own up to your wounds and ask God for help in bearing them, you will not be tempted to blame God for not working a miracle. You must remember that our God is a God of death *and* resurrection.

You do have an obligation to attempt reconciliation after separation; but if, after proper counseling, your attempts fail, you can rest assured that you have done what you could. Often, even your sincere efforts only prolong the affliction. And those who succeed in reconciling frequently discover that nothing has changed. "All I am is older, but no wiser."

Resignation

The fourth stage is that of *resignation:* "Yes me, this is happening to me." The daydreaming (the wishing to be somewhere else) begins to disappear. Resignation is hard to arrive at; even when attained, it is easily abandoned for one of the earlier stages. If you have not adequately lived through the earlier stages, resignation can quickly become depression, as you turn in upon yourself those bitter and helpless feelings.

You begin to see yourself as divorced; and with that realization you no longer feel set apart from the rest of the world. You have admitted the fact of your separation and divorce to your parents, neighbors, friends, and people at work. The dust has finally begun to settle. Having sorted out your life, you now begin to fit the pieces into place.

You must, however, be prepared for a change of moods; your high may suddenly change to a low. As the denial, the anger, and the bargaining wind down, the numbness may give way to fright and despair. "How am I going to make it?" "What do I have to live for?" Thoughts of suicide may enter your mind. As your life reaches its lowest ebb, all reasons to go on living seem to evaporate, and death by your own hand may seem to be the only answer. Holidays are especially irksome. "Everyone else seems to be close to others and to be happy. I'm so alone and no one seems to care." After the joyful moments of Christmas day, late that same night one woman stood in her kitchen, which was in terrible disarray. Her ex-husband had taken their children back to his motel room and she was left with the mess. How extremely depressed she felt. The state of her kitchen reflected the state of her emotions.

Usually, a heart-to-heart talk with a friend or several sessions with a competent counselor can get you over the severe hump. Eventually, you will learn how *to pick yourself up* from such depression. As time goes on, this will happen more readily. You must try to avoid too many highs, since the only direction you can take from a high is a low; and this leads to depression. One woman came home from her divorce hearing and immediately played Barbra Streisand's song "Free Again." Over and over she listened to it. She was in ecstasy. For the first time in years she was finally "free again." Yet, when she shut off the record hours later, she went into a severe depression and cried all night. Your period of resignation must become a time of balance. As you start to take charge of your life, you must do so without allowing the circumstances of life to knock you off balance. Your goal at this stage is to keep an even keel. You have just weathered a tremendous storm. Your most important task is to stay afloat.

Acceptance

The fifth stage, *acceptance,* points you toward finding new anchors in your life. You have reached the acceptance stage when you no longer dwell on the past or dream about the future. Rather, you can live and enjoy the present moment. You do not bury your feelings; you express them willingly. You are at acceptance when you leave the treadmill — to walk and run on your own. You are enjoying your life, and are learning to deal with it as it presents itself. You replace your fears with the excitement of making a new beginning. "It was very hard to leave my children at school and go off so many miles to work. But a whole new world has opened up for me. Before, I was living life in black and white. Now, it's in living color. I enjoy going out to lunch every day and meeting old friends as well as making new ones."

At the point of acceptance, you are no longer afraid to see yourself as a single person. It's OK to be single. Being lonely at times is not the worst fate in the world. The acceptance stage is usually a long time in coming. But it eventually will arrive if you are willing to *pass through* these normal stages of grief. Your inclination, of course, is to try to bypass the grief, to go from denial or anger to acceptance, in order to avoid the agony.

As a child, when you bought a box of Cracker Jack you turned it over and opened up the bottom to get at the prize. You were unwilling *to go through* the nuts and the corn to arrive at the prize. You wanted — right now — to have what was beneath it all. As an adult (who happens to be divorced), you have the same desire — to arrive at the stage of acceptance without first passing through the other stages. Doing it that way, sad to say, rarely will achieve the outcome you seek.

It should also be remembered that these grief stages do not always follow one another chronologically. You may experience denial and bargaining at the same time; you may go from resignation to anger; you may be at acceptance over several aspects of the separation, but at denial or anger over other aspects.

These stages can recur from time to time and not necessarily in the same order. You may arrive at acceptance (really feeling that you are your old self again) only to be informed that your former spouse is getting remarried, and suddenly you're back to square two — the anger stage. You pray that your return to one of these stages, even though very severe and traumatic, will not be as long-lasting as the previous time.

"See the light at the end of the tunnel? I sure have. This was a long time in coming, too. Then when I think that I'm home free and about out of my dark tunnel, another train I wasn't looking for comes by and rolls over me. But I'm still going."

4
What About the Children?

"How am *I* going to survive?" This is the primary question that you mulled over as you went through the separation and divorce. You were thinking about Number One — *yourself*. This is only natural since at the time it is a matter of survival. Everyone else becomes secondary to your own self-preservation.

Next comes your work. As a man, you may have to find a better-paying job. As a woman, you will have to find a well-paying job to relieve the financial needs of your family. If there is a third party involved, this person will receive much of your attention. Only then are the children considered. You do not willfully intend to hurt them. In fact, many times the divorce is sought so that the family life will become more stable and meaningful. Yet, sufficient dialogue with the children is frequently missing.

Just as you go through the five stages of grief described in the last chapter, so do your children go through them in their own way.

At the *denial* stage, for your children, the separation or the divorce is a "big secret" that they hope their friends and their teachers will not discover. Where once they had entertained their friends at home, they are now frightened to do this. They do not view their house as their "home" any longer since one parent is gone. They are afraid that if their friends come over, they might ask about the missing parent and they would be most embarrassed to tell them the truth. Your children perceive you as angry, sullen, and weepy; and rather than say anything, they withdraw further into a shell of denial.

The *anger* stage manifests itself in a number of ways: your children fight with their brothers and sisters or playmates; they have little or no desire to concentrate and study, thereby resulting in a drop in grades. They may lash out at you as mother, blaming you for causing their father to leave, when you may not have been the primary cause at all. But since you are the one close at hand, you bear the brunt of their anger.

You, as a visiting father, may be on the receiving end of your children's repressed anger. They may not want to visit you; they may refuse to eat, study, or take discipline from you. They are acting out the way that they feel.

When children see that you are more concerned with yourself than with them, they display anger in order to get more attention. This is normal. Or, in some cases, children will repress their anger and refuse to cry because they see you crying or looking upset. They don't want to add to your misery, and they think they are helping you by repressing their emotions.

Bargaining is natural for children of divorced parents — unless their homelife is so unfit that they long for a change. They may cry, plead, whine, run away, or do almost anything to reunite their parents. "I'll be good; just let Daddy come back home." "If I do all my chores and eat my spinach, can we try and be a family again?"

Usually, young children are unaware of the problem caused by a third party involved with either parent. Nor can they grasp the deep-rooted, unresolvable problems that continue to exist. Thus your children cannot comprehend why many of the difficulties they see cannot be resolved. They spend much of their time hoping and praying that a reunion will take place. These are not their reactions, of course, where there has been undue turmoil, quarreling, and extreme physical abuse.

Resignation begins to happen when the dust settles, when quarreling is at a minimum and when the intense loyalties of the children to either mother or father begin to level off. Generally, the children show care and concern about both parents. As order and tranquillity are reestablished in the home and new patterns of daily living are set up for eating, getting to school, visiting a friend after school, the children become resigned to this new life. Their prayers have not been answered, but they do experience a kind of peace and quiet that was previously missing.

Children do look forward to being with the absent parent. They have much fun at visitation time. "My life's OK. It sure is great having it quiet at home. It's neat to have my dad play with me on the weekends."

Children reach the *acceptance* stage when they realize that they are not the only ones in the world whose parents are separated and divorced. In some schools or classrooms, twenty-five to fifty percent or more of the children are having similar family experiences. This is not a case of misery loving company, but of recognition of their identity and receiving support. They are adjusting to the fact that they are not the only ones in the world coming from a divorced home. In time, they will accept your divorce and the scars will heal. More and more they will recognize that they have *their own lives* to lead and this is of the utmost importance.

"I always assumed that family meant mother, father, and children. With all of the anger and the fighting going on, we have hardly been a family for a long time. Now I see that family is built on love, even if one family member does not live with us. As we love and care for one another, we are much more of a family than the people across the street who don't get along at all."

After Acceptance

Children have the capacity to manipulate their parents in the best of homes, and such is the case in most homes where the parents are separated. Consistency in discipline together with moral upbringing are necessary, even though the two parents are living apart. You can accomplish this by gently closing the door on the former marriage and, yet, very much leaving open the door of being a parent.

It is essential as a parent to continue to talk with your former spouse about the children, their growth pattern and their needs. The children still must be cared for and loved. This can be done after the dust has settled and the other doors on the marriage have been gently closed.

The loss of you as a full-time parent is usually a traumatic experience for your children. Without a doubt, you and your former spouse are the two most important people in their lives; and your presence is essential to their development as persons. When one parent departs, his or her influence is thereby lessened, and this causes an emotional upheaval in the children. Because of this, they will often cling to you for fear that you, too, will leave them. Continual assurances of love, care, and support by you and your former spouse are much needed.

Given your continued love and attention, no permanent scars or effects are likely to stay with your children. If anything, they are likely to be more adept at handling crises and life's uncertainties than children coming from homes where the parents are living together. There is more than one way to define the word *family*.

5
Learning to Trust Again

Divorce, by its very nature, has a shattering effect on the family itself. But what it does to the *trust* of the individual spouse is even worse. In full faith you entrusted yourself to another human being, promising to love that person "in good times and in bad . . . all the days of my life." Now—after years of fathering and mothering, of changing jobs to better support the family, of dedicating yourself to the countless tasks of homemaking — your marriage no longer exists. Can you ever trust anyone again?

Divorce has shattered the uniquely precious vase of your marriage, and you must now begin to pick up the pieces. Stricken to the core, you complain: "Who in the world is there left to trust?" "All men are. . . ." "All women are. . . ." And because of your past hurts you avoid close contacts with others. You might even want to withdraw into your own shell: "After our divorce I was left with a family of three teenagers. Distraught, I decided to withdraw into the basement of our home. I felt secure there, away from everybody and everything. Months went by. My children managed somehow. Safe in my retreat, I did my own washing and ironing. I even cooked for myself — when I felt like eating. Then one day my oldest son came down, put his arm around me, and said: 'It's OK, Mom, you can come up now.' As I walked up those stairs, I felt like I was reentering life once again."

Trust Yourself

A lack of trust in others is basically a lack of trust in yourself. You do not trust others because you do not trust yourself. Your ego, your self has been shattered. Only you can put your self back together again.

After the separation and the divorce you will tend to mistrust your own judgment: "I did everything by the book — a long courtship, no premarital sex, a church wedding — and I stayed faithful throughout the marriage, the whole bit. It got me nowhere."

"I'm so confused on what to do. Should I be strict with the kids or give them their way? Should I accept this job offer or not? Should I go to the party or not?"

During your marriage you made many choices that you truly believed were valid and good; but now — after a divorce — you begin to wonder. And, as a result, you lack confidence in your present decisions about life. Such a lack of confidence in personal decisions comes from that deep inner feeling of failure. "Our marriage failed; therefore, I am a failure."

Most likely, whatever decisions you made in your marriage were the right ones *at the time* that you made them. And, taken singly, they could not be the only cause of your divorce: "Moving into a new home did unsettle our homelife, but all of the problems were already lying there like booby traps, ready to be triggered at the slightest misstep."

"My becoming pregnant in the face of all our other problems did not cause the breakup. We just couldn't handle the other pressures. Besides, that child is the biggest joy in my life today."

Many, if not all, of the decisions you made were the right ones. And it does you no good to look back. Hindsight, always twenty-twenty, only causes undue anguish.

After divorce, you need to believe in yourself more than ever before. Your belief in God should help you here. Although you may feel a sense of personal failure, self-pity, and lack of trust, your past decisions must have worked reasonably well; your past accomplishments are proof of that. In time you will recognize more fully that you have come a long way in your life, even if you do not believe it at this moment.

Make Decisions

It can be disconcerting to reach out to others after the separation or divorce and find that you cannot trust them. You discover, for example, that someone you thought was a friend is really no friend at all. Taking advantage of another is not a sign of friendship. Such an experience will force you to take an even deeper, more penetrating look at yourself. Positive statements of self-trust are often long in coming, but are most necessary: "Now that the divorce is final, everyone in the family is finally settled and all seem much happier than they have been in years."

"I was still in a daze when I took this job, but it has been a real growth opportunity for me every step of the way."

"I dreaded the move, but now that I am unpacked, I like it here."

"At the time of the separation and the divorce, I was so miserable. My ex-spouse seemed so calm and content, it aggravated me to no end. Now I'm more together with my life than my ex-spouse."

"I decided to be firm with my discipline of the children and to temper it with love. They are really coming out of the doldrums."

"I've hated filling the shoes of my ex-spouse. But I am so proud of myself when my supper is tasty, my checkbook almost balances, and the kitchen has a clean smell about it."

"I have finally allowed myself the freedom to make a few mistakes and to fail. I am making decisions on my own."

The above statements prove that you have many hidden resources and strengths yet to tap. God gave you all the tools you need, not only to survive but to overcome the gloomiest aspects of your separation and divorce. Only one person in the world can defeat you, and that is you yourself.

After you learn to trust yourself and make your own decisions it will be less difficult to trust others. But remember that you are very vulnerable while the wounds of your divorce are still open and sore. You could get hurt, but you could also form a friendship just when you need it the most.

You may wonder about a person who seems to be using you. If your wonder turns to suspicion and that suspicion is borne out, then you will have to close yet another door and move on. Just be sure that you do not enjoy being used, that you do not suffer from a doormat neurosis. Your self-image may still need a lot of attention.

You may be tempted to be promiscuous or to live with another person with no thought of a permanent commitment. Beneath your many outer layers you are terrified of being harmed as you were in your marriage. But in trying to avoid this you know that you are skating on thin ice, and that is not really living at all.

Obtaining a divorce forces you to do a lot of serious thinking. Surely you have asked yourself: "Where will I be a year from now? five years from now?" Such a question is unfair, of course, because no one can determine *where* he or she will be a year or five years from now. Only God knows that. The real question to ask is this: "*Who* will I be a year from now? five years from now?" This is completely within your power to determine. For you can use God's graces to make yourself a more loving, open, sensitive, and trusting person. Who you are to be, you are now becoming.

6
Your Need for Caring Love

Of all God's creatures, we alone have been given the ability to care. A skinned knee — a mother cares. A grandfather dying of cancer — a family cares. A flat tire — a stranger cares. A devastating earthquake — a world cares. We have many pursuits in life, but perhaps our most profound quest is to find someone who genuinely cares about us.

As you endured your separation and divorce, you surely must have thought to yourself: "Does anybody care about me? Does anybody *really* care about me?" And as you slumped deeper into depression — in despair at the loss of your self-worth — you no doubt thought: "Why should anybody care about me? I'm a failure." But such thoughts only build walls around you and keep people away. Denial, as was seen in chapter 3, prevents others from showing that they care.

Caring is built on the physical and the spiritual presence of others. "I'm here when you need me. I'm here even when you don't need me. I care." As you experience your separation and divorce, there will be many expressions of caring genuinely manifested. In time your eyes will see them more clearly.

- A bulletin about a rap group for the divorced. *Somebody cares!*
- An invitation to a party where you'll feel comfortable. *Somebody cares!*
- A phone call from a friend to say, "Hello." *Somebody cares!*

- A dinner invitation from some married friends. *Somebody cares!*
- A free babysitting offer so you can have the night out. *Somebody cares!*
- A clergyman who stops to ask how you feel and how you are doing. *Somebody cares!*
- A neighbor who cleans your sidewalk after there is a full night of snow. *Somebody cares!*
- A doctor who spends an extra fifteen minutes helping to heal your inner self. *Somebody cares!*
- A boss who daily asks, "How are you doing today?" *Somebody cares!*
- A member of the opposite sex who is interested in you and not just interested in playing games. *Somebody cares!*
- A shoulder to lean on and to cry on. *Somebody cares!*

Good Samaritans

"There was a man going down from Jerusalem to Jericho who fell prey to robbers. They stripped him, beat him, and then went off leaving him half-dead. A priest happened to be going down the same road; he saw him but continued on. Likewise there was a Levite who came the same way; he saw him and went on. But a Samaritan who was journeying along came on him and was moved to pity at the sight. He approached him and dressed his wounds, pouring in oil and wine. He then hoisted him on his own beast and brought him to an inn, where he cared for him. The next day he took out two silver pieces and gave them to the innkeeper with the request: 'Look after him, and if there is any further expense I will repay you on my way back.'

"Which of these three, in your opinion, was neighbor to the man who fell in with the robbers?" The answer came, "The one who treated him with compassion." Jesus said to him, "Then go and do the same" (Luke 10:30-37).

Lying helpless in the middle of the road, no one seeming to care, everyone passing by, and you dying — does this sound familiar? That is the way you feel now after your separation and divorce. You know about Levites, especially your family and friends who took a look and continued on their way. They could not understand. They were afraid. They showed pity but not compassion. They saw you as a threat to their marriage. They passed by.

Your priest or minister — interested in saving your marriage but not sure about how to help you — may have passed you by. He surely wanted to help you, but he may have been unfamiliar with how to deal with you as half of a couple.

A good Samaritan is someone who cares. Parents can show you their affection by lending support, without demanding control. They can become closer to their grandchildren and help guide them through difficult times. "I never knew what great parents I had. They tried to understand, to love the both of us. They took their grandchildren all summer while I tried to sort out my future."

Neighbors who in the past rarely offered more than a casual "Hello," may dig out a snowed-in automobile or volunteer to watch the children at a moment's notice. Going next door for coffee and compassion brings relief during many a lonely evening. "During the initial grief stages, I went next door several times a week, even after midnight. Frank and June listened to my tale of woe over and over and never seemed to mind."

Good Samaritans can also be found at your place of work. A sensitive boss can make all the difference in the world. Realizing the trauma and the pain, a good Samaritan boss will allow you time off to make a court appearance, to sell your house, to recover from a depressing weekend, or to take care of a child who is sick.

Sensing what must be going on at home, good Samaritan co-workers can be tolerant and caring — by letting you know that you are more important than your given task. They reach out to you during a coffee break: "Are you sure that you are

OK?'' or "You are burying yourself in your work. Why not try to stop running for the rest of today?"

Priests and ministers are usually good Samaritans. For every one who may have passed you by in the middle of the road, countless others will go out of their way to care for you. They possess the Lord's power to heal and comfort you and help lift you up from the depths of despair. A five-minute call or a half-hour conference with one of God's allies can help you to turn the tide on a gloomy day and leave you saying, "I can make it."

Of course, there will be those who are not good Samaritans at all. Under pretense of caring for you, they will try to change you or make you into somebody else: "Why love the bum? Look what he did to you." "Forget her. The bars are loaded with women who would just love to get their hands on you." This kind of advice pays little heed to the fact that you feel like you've just failed in the most important assignment in your life.

Friend: "Find thirty people with whom you can share when the going gets rough."
You: "I don't know thirty people on whose shoulders I can cry every time that I have a need."
Friend: "Then find two really special people you can go to and share with them fifteen times each."

There are such people out there — people who will accept you with your faults (your smoking and drinking habits, your forgetfulness, your moods, your flare-ups, your laziness, and your inconsistencies). Of course, you don't have all those faults, but you are probably in there somewhere. When some special person accepts you just as you are, you will begin to see the light at the end of your tunnel.

Caring Love

Christ cared for people as he found them — a woman writhing under an accusation of adultery, the apostles stewing because they had not caught any fish all night, the people feeling hunger after following him all day, or the children clamoring to receive his blessing at the end of an exhausting day. He tried to raise them all a little bit higher. Jesus overlooked specific faults and concentrated on the overall mosaic of the person as any good friend would do. That same Christ is present in your life.

What you need from others at this time is *caring* love. This kind of love creates no dependencies, has no strings attached, and is totally unconditional. Unlike erotic love which can be described as reaction to stimulus and is, therefore, self-centered, caring love is a personal response to the worth of another and is, therefore, other-person oriented.

In seeking this caring love after your separation and divorce you will have to make some adjustments in your sex life. Sex was always integral to your marriage; it unified, healed, and sustained you. Now you will be tempted to vacillate between two extremes: You will avoid encounters with the opposite sex because they are too painful to your wounded self; or you will become obsessed with sex, not even trying to seek out a caring-love relationship.

"How can I live without sex after years of having it in marriage?" Before that question can be answered, another must be asked: "Am I (presuming that I will eventually be free to remarry) ready to love again? Am I ready to trust another, to give of myself completely and unconditionally? Am I willing to commit myself to another person? Am I ready to care about one, single person again?" If the answer is *"No,"* or there is hesitation or the need for qualification, then you are only playing games with sex, no matter how you try to rationalize your needs or your maturity. Sex soon becomes usury.

Sexual feelings are extremely powerful; they are as strong as any that you possess. But, just as in marriage you had to control them — when your spouse was absent or when it was the wrong time — so now you must learn to discipline yourself.

When you are not cared for, you become lonely. But loneliness is not the worst feeling in the world. Everyone gets lonely, from the president in the White House to the patient in a hospital bed. You are not alone. Think back to how lonely you felt even at times when your marriage was going relatively well. Check out for yourself the why of your present loneliness. Is it the holiday season? Is it a lack of self-worth you feel? Are you afraid of being alone? Once you discover the reason, you may be able to respond to your loneliness in a way other than a sexual encounter.

"The singles bars and the social clubs all turned out to be meat markets. When I looked elsewhere, I found that I could care again. I still get lonely. But I've got a friend to share with and my friend does care."

You will reach a point where you can be alone without being lonely. You will come to enjoy and savor your aloneness with the peace and tranquillity it brings you. Your loneliness will be a void that you will learn to fill with new friends and old, with experiences that you never knew existed during the time when you were married. Your new life will eventually mean more time alone rather than more lonely time.

The Church as Good Samaritan

You may wonder whether the Church has changed her position on sexual morality. In her doctrines, the Church has not changed. In her sensitivity and her caring for the individual Christian who struggles with his or her own sexuality, the Church opens her arms wide to heal you and alleviate your pain. Through her traditional teachings, the Church is not trying to stifle you; rather, through her ministers she is attempting to help you grow into a *caring* kind of love. And to arrive at that objective you need guidelines to protect you from harming yourself and others.

"I thought for the longest time that the Church was being unduly rigid and harsh with her teachings on sex and morality.

But from my experience in lounges and with certain social clubs, I could see the value of our traditional teachings. Streets need stop signs and traffic lights. And life needs guideposts to point the way." It has been said that the human animal is the only animal that can say "No." But to make such a decision requires a conscience formed by definite guidelines.

In some dioceses, permission to seek a civil divorce must be requested from the bishop; so, you should consult with your parish priest. You may continue to receive the sacraments. If you remarry outside the Catholic Church, you are not allowed to receive the sacraments. In this latter case, however, you should consult with a priest to see if anything can be done.

To show her care and concern for the faithful, the Catholic Church in the United States has established matrimonial tribunals in each diocese. The purpose of a tribunal is to help the divorced and remarried person, the divorced person intending another marriage, and the divorced Catholic seeking a clarification of his or her standing in the Church. This help consists of information and recommendations which at times will lead to an annulment process.

The Church presumes that if two baptized Christian believers marry and consummate their union, their marriage is sacramental and, therefore, cannot be dissolved by any earthly power. But if evidence can be amassed to prove that presumption wrong, the Church can annul the marriage. The Church also presumes that the bride and groom are capable of making a real matrimonial contract. But, because of our new understanding of human nature provided by the behavioral sciences, the Church now realizes that this capability is not always exercised at the marriage ceremony. Grounds for annulment in this area include such reasons as psychological incapacity or immaturity, lack of due discretion or of true marital commitment. So, if investigation shows that something essential for a true marriage was lacking, the tribunal can declare that a sacramental bond never existed in the first place. This is called a declaration of nullity.

An annulment granted by the Catholic Church does not deny that a real relationship existed; nor does it imply that the relationship was entered with ill will or moral fault. It does not make your children illegitimate in any sense. And, to satisfy legal requirements, it must be preceded by a civil divorce. Either of the former spouses may file for the annulment and once it is granted, it applies to both of the parties.

Catholics generally petition for an annulment so that they can feel spiritually free of their first union. As a Catholic who may want to remarry, you know this is impossible unless you and your intended spouse are free to remarry both in the eyes of the State and in the eyes of the Church. Be assured that Catholic matrimonial tribunals will keep all annulment proceedings in strict confidence.

In most dioceses of the country, the annulment process takes about one year or more. Information must be gathered, witnesses must be interviewed — and the volume of cases continues to grow. Any priest can initiate your annulment proceedings. He will work through his diocesan matrimonial tribunal. You will probably be asked to help defray the cost of processing your annulment, but this should not deter you from seeking it since arrangements can be made for expenses.

You may feel that an annulment is no different from a divorce. Not so. It is a declaration by the Church that a man and woman never entered into a true Christian marriage. And in this way the Catholic Church very much upholds the sanctity of marriage.

If you are a Catholic and need counseling about your divorce and a possible annulment, do see a priest. He can be a good Samaritan to you by pointing out a new way of life and by aiding you in your spiritual healing.

7
What to Do About Guilt Feelings

Purveyors of a new kind of life-style have proclaimed during the past two decades that guilt is the onus that organized religion places on people in order to exercise control over them. Without such imposed guilt, they say, people would be free human beings and not psychological misfits, weighed down by so many hangups. "If it feels good, do it!" has become the philosophy of many people in today's world. Thus they try to brush aside any feelings of guilt.

Yet, all of life is made up of a pattern, an order, a certain fabric. Mores and morality are part of this fabric of life. When you go against this order and violate the essence of your own existence, you feel guilty, and rightfully so. Societies and religions have long recognized these life-preserving and life-ordering patterns of human life; and they have taught, encouraged, and sometimes imposed these on their people. But the source of this order comes originally from within. (See Jeremiah 31:33.) Thus were you fashioned by the hand of your Creator.

Guilt is often present in the breakup of a marriage relationship. "Look at what suffering I've caused my spouse, the children, my parents, and my in-laws by what I've done." The admission of guilt is a healthy experience, like dealing with grief. Denial of guilt or any wrongdoing or any personal part in the disrupting of the homelife results in unresolved tensions which in time will have to be resolved. The ultimate judge is neither a court of law nor any external laws or mores; it lies within the heart — ''What did *I* really do?'' ''What did *I* really say?'' Whether you belong to the presently married or to the formerly married, you must still live with yourself.

To say ''I don't feel guilty about our marriage breakup'' may well be a true statement. You may have had little to do with the final break, and your conscience may be fairly clear. Yet, deep-rooted guilt feelings are often buried beneath the surface. Eventually, these feelings need to be expressed.

''I kept taking him back all the time, refusing to admit that he had problems, problems that were not going to be solved for a long, long time. The longer I stayed in that situation, the more I became part of the problem. I feel so guilty for not having taken a stand much earlier. I put myself and the poor kids through so much agony for so many years.''

''For years all I've been doing is running. Running with my job, seeking promotions, and in effect, not dealing with my wife and what or wasn't going on at home. Paying more attention to my job than to my family has been my way of life, and I feel so guilty.''

Psychologically and spiritually, it is therapeutic to sort out your life and your guilt. Once guilt is exposed it can be dealt with and life can go forward. But in doing so it is necessary to distinguish between *realistic* guilt and *unrealistic* guilt.

Realistic Guilt

Realistic guilt results from those actions or words for which you are truly responsible — games acted out, profanity, open hostility, cheating, jealousy, drinking, physical abuse, and so on. These actions are contrary to your ideal life pattern. They cause a gnawing and an eating away. They are much like cancer, which can be present for years but not known or attended to until it is about to bring life to a halt. Guilt is a spiritual cancer whose presence is unknown to you until it practically shuts down your life. Realistic guilt is based on fact;

and because it is actual it can be admitted, dealt with, and forgiven. But admission is often difficult, because it makes you assess yourself and stop pretending. Once you admit your guilt you are ready to take the following steps.

First, you will *forgive yourself*, as you realize that you are fallible and weak, that you make mistakes, and that you are capable of sinning. Not dealing with guilt means taking it out on yourself: "Why me? Why me all the time?" or "You stupid idiot, how could you?" Forgiving yourself means resolving the past — the ancient past or the past as recent as this morning. It means saying to yourself in the mirror: "Hey, you, I'm sorry."

Next, you will *forgive others*. You should express your sorrow to your former spouse, the children, anyone who has been harmed. Sometimes it is impossible to reach the ones offended; they have moved to faraway places or have passed away. You may still pray to God for their forgiveness.

Finally, you will *seek forgiveness from God* through a priest or minister. A Catholic, for example, knows quite well that reception of the sacrament of Reconciliation heals the soul and lifts a tremendous weight off the shoulders. God touches your inner life with his grace and once again you are a whole person.

This is the process for resolving your realistic guilt — forgiving yourself, seeking forgiveness from others, and finally, begging pardon from God. All three are necessary for you to become fully alive again. Love *does* mean having to say you're sorry.

Unrealistic Guilt

Unrealistic guilt derives from those marriage miseries that you did not cause or for which you were only slightly responsible. A woman may say: "Look what I caused by filing for a divorce . . . I broke up our family." And she says this despite the fact that her husband drank excessively, beat her regularly, and belittled the children frequently.

A man may say: "I filed for divorce, and she's had one affair after another. I feel so guilty about having filed." But her affairs are her own responsibility and not his at all. Counselors often ask the question: "Who owns the problem?" This question of ownership of the problem applies here. But to answer it requires great discernment.

Most of us have a tendency to be hard on ourselves, to heap blame and guilt on ourselves for everything that goes wrong in a given situation. With the many loose ends present in a marital breakup, guilt is the tip of each frayed end.

Unrealistic guilt can be lethal. Financial difficulties, your children's problems, your former spouse engaging in self-destructive activities, your suffering parents — these are some of the crises that may follow your separation and divorce. Yet, you may not be directly responsible for any of them. Even in happy homes, finances are rarely ever stable, children have their problems, and parents tend to shout "Disgrace," even as Adam and Eve did about Cain and Abel.

Unrealistic guilt cannot be resolved. And this is so because you cannot properly delineate the actual causes of the effects which you see. There are so many gray areas. Sometimes even what God has created and what men have manufactured do not live up to our expectations. Rolls Royces stall; hurricanes hit tropical paradises; and marriages die. All of this and so much more happens every day with no one reason that can be pointed to for an adequate explanation.

Your parents and teachers have impressed upon you that all of life has an answer. For years you were graded on your answers. But now — after your divorce — you are faced with many unanswered questions. You may never find an adequate explanation for your divorce. You may well have to live the rest of your life without knowing the real reasons why your marriage broke up.

But attempting to live with unrealistic guilt is life-defeating; it is like trying to play baseball without a bat or a ball. You must, of course, take on the burdens you personally and truly caused. The rest of the problems must be solved by the person (or persons) responsible for them.

Make a List

It can be most helpful to write out your realistic and unrealistic guilts. As you see your realistic guilts on paper, you learn to forgive yourself, and you can plan how to seek forgiveness from others and from God. And when you examine your unrealistic guilts — seeing them for what they really are — you can more easily determine how to rid yourself of them.

Here is the way these lists might look.

Unrealistic Guilt

- My son getting D's this semester
- My filing for divorce which broke up our family life
- My compulsive worrying about the stigma of my divorce
- Having my in-laws dislike me
- Causing my elderly father to get sick
- All of the "If onlys"
  If only . . .
  I had stopped seeing my former spouse after the first date.
  I had not put myself and my family through all of this turmoil.
  I had accepted counseling or had gone to counseling sooner.
  I had done more to save the marriage.
  I had made our sex life more pleasurable.
  I had gone to church more often.
  I had not been so wrapped up in my job and material things.

Realistic Guilt

- I was unfaithful to my spouse during our marriage.
- I was not responsive to my spouse and the children.
- I neglected the children in order to take care of my own needs.
- I unnecessarily made the divorce proceedings an ugly mess.

- I cut off my former spouse, my parents, and old friends right in the middle of telephone conversations.
- I took out my own anger and frustration on the children by screaming at them, disciplining them unjustly, demanding too much from them, and even hitting them.
- I slandered my former spouse by the things I told other people.
- I dwelt constantly on the past.
- I used alcohol and other drugs excessively.
- I stopped going to church, and I didn't take the children to church either.
- I spent an excessive amount of time in bars and lounges.

Once your two lists are completed, deal first with your unrealistic guilts. Be sure that you have a complete list of your "If onlys."

Then take your list of realistic guilts and add the following words wherever they can be inserted: I was wrong . . . I am sorry . . . I forgive myself . . . I pray that he/she will forgive me . . . I beg God's forgiveness. Here is an example: "I was wrong for being unfaithful during our marriage. I am sorry. I forgive myself. I pray that my former spouse and my family will forgive me. I beg God's forgiveness." Do this for each of your realistic guilts. This way you will own your guilt and you will thereby resolve it.

"Love makes the world go round." Is this really true in your life? Or does guilt make your world go round? Stop and consider what motivates your words and actions. How many are said and done because of love welling up within you? How many are said and done because you would feel guilty otherwise? Motivate your life with love, and your guilt will disappear.

8
Close the Door Gently

Although a marriage may die officially when two people separate and divorce, the relationship between the couple still exists. This relationship continues in various ways — through sharing with the children on weekends and holidays, and alimony or support payments made at the specified times. Then, too, weddings, anniversaries, sicknesses, deaths, graduations, etc. usually require continued contact.

Even when there are no children or when the former spouse has moved elsewhere, there are hopes, fantasies, and memories that remain. One wife, after many years of no contact with her former husband, admitted that she did not get in touch with him because she was afraid that he had remarried. She was unwilling to face this possibility.

Since the marriage has died while leaving the relationship alive, you need to "close the door gently," neither slamming it shut nor leaving it ajar. "Closing the door gently" begins with taking stock of what the marriage was and was not, seeing your former spouse as neither a hero or a bum, a saint or a witch, and then gently shutting off your emotions, feelings of love or of hate or of both.

If you are to make a new beginning after separation and divorce, there has to be a gentle closing of the door behind you. Before a new owner can move into a home, the previous owners must give up claim to it. So, too, your former marriage must be discontinued softly and gently if your life is to continue smoothly.

Don't Slam the Door

The anger and the bitterness spoken of in earlier chapters may cause you to slam the door on your marriage with great violence. Your whole life shaken by what has happened, you and your children feel like you are living in limbo (or in hell). What was once your home is now a shambles. It is so easy for you to be both angry and bitter.

The danger of slamming any door is the harm that can come to an arm, a leg, or even a head. Great emotional and physical suffering can result. The initial hurt over the origins of the divorce — infidelity, alcoholism, gambling, irresponsibility, abusiveness, physical cruelty — continues to cause anguish. The breakup of the marriage and the home, as well as the guilt, cause the spouses to lash out at each other.

Much hostility is directed at the spouse who enters a new marriage. This terminates whatever subliminal hopes were still alive in the other spouse. And the door slams firmly shut. One has somebody and the other has nobody.

You may be tempted to play games through your lawyers. The door keeps slamming. Injury follows injury, "I'll show you . . . I'll show you!"

The telephone is frequently used for slamming purposes — calling at all hours and then hanging up, using abusive language, slamming the phone down, calling when extremely depressed, lonely, or intoxicated.

The stages of grief spoken of in chapter 3 may also cause problems at this time. Today you may be feeling the acceptance of your separation and divorce. Tomorrow after a phone call or a visit from your former spouse you may feel bitter and resentful, or you may begin to bargain once more. Just when you find that you have ceased slamming the door, your ex-spouse may remarry or get abusive, upset the children, or in some way trigger feelings you thought you had buried. As a child, your parents told you to stop slamming the door. As an adult, you still have to keep this in mind.

Don't Leave the Door Ajar

Extreme loneliness, depression, and a personal sense of failure occur with the death of your marriage. At times these almost consume you in misery. These can become so excessive that drinking, adultery, and attempted suicide become very inviting. Such personal pressure can cause the door separating you and your former spouse to remain open. The separation or divorce can be more than you bargained for or more than you can cope with at present. So you leave the door ajar. "Somehow we will get back together again. As bad as the marriage was, the aftermath is as bad or worse."

Your former spouse may come for a visit and ask to stay overnight, tarry after dropping off the children, call with hopes of reconciliation, send gifts or flowers, and even create false hopes in the children. Any or all of the above may occur after the formal divorce or even after one or both have remarried.

Because of all this pressure, you may be tempted to renew your attempts at reconciliation. But if this did not work after your separation when — after much counseling — you both failed to settle your differences after taking a hard look at your problems, then it can scarcely happen now.

After your divorce you are extremely vulnerable. For this reason, any halfhearted attempts at reconciliation only produce a greater internal turmoil. Just when a healing is starting to happen and a new life is beginning, these attempts to salvage "what might have been" only diminish what emotional progress has been made.

Even so, you may still feel that somehow, some way the two of you will be reunited. But this attitude tries to skirt the humanness of the marriage and the two people involved — their shortcomings and their failures. For years, you may continue to fantasize about a future reunion. You just don't want to get on with your life after your divorce.

Such things can happen even years later. One divorcee was thought to be a perfect model in this area of adjustment. She had raised her children well, and she seemed so vibrant and happy. But one day, some fifteen years after her divorce, she was seen weeping at her office desk. Distinctly she could be heard saying over and over, "Where is he now that I really need him?" A serious operation was in the offing for her. A door had been left ajar and a new life had not truly begun. So after fifteen years her thoughts and emotions went back to her former spouse.

When you leave a door open in your home, you feel a draft which often results in a cold. When you leave open the door to your already dead marriage, you may never fully recover from the chilling consequences.

Close the Door Gently

Closing the door gently on your marriage means that you continue to direct your life through the grief process and its recurring stages. It means grabbing a firm hold of the knob and gently pushing the door shut. You must be willing to accept your present state, with its financial worries, concerns over the children, feelings of loneliness and aloneness.

There has to be a true *letting go* of your former spouse no matter what the future holds for either of you. Life is no longer a partnership but a single undertaking. This means that you will have to face the loss of your house (depending on the court settlement), exclusive rights to the children, and the other losses listed in chapter 2. Your feelings of love and even of concern must be translated into feelings of respect and good will and friendship. Your feelings of hate and bitterness must also give way to those of forgiveness and compassion.

You must be willing to say good-bye and to live in accord with your words. Once your marriage is over, there is no going back, no matter how distressing the present might be for you. Besides your own life, many other lives (your children, parents, in-laws, employees, friends, and others) are involved in your decision. These lives, too, need to go on. Once good-byes are said at the airport, the plane takes off. The pilot cannot turn back just because you have changed your mind about flying. You must stay on the plane until it arrives at your destination. There is no turning back. The same must be true as you close the door gently on your marriage and take off for new horizons.

All this, of course, is not easy to do. But here are seven suggested ways to make it less difficult for you to make a new beginning in life.

Look Ahead, Not Behind

Why look back? Why not look ahead? In doing so you will see that you are really moving somewhere with your life, even if it is at a snail's pace. Look ahead to tomorrow. There is no future in yesterday.

Light Up the Darkness

Many children are afraid of the dark. But usually they outgrow their fear. So will you outgrow the fear of the darkness that surrounds you after your divorce. Smile, even if you have to force it. Light up your life by helping some other person. This stops you from dwelling on yourself and your problems. It gives worth to your life.

Decide on How You Want to Live

In your life after divorce, you are faced with many decisions on how you want to live. If you believe down deep that you are worthless, you will tend to withdraw from life. If you work too hard at being busy, you are trying to escape the reality of life. You are not worthless; be assured of that. Nor can overwork help you to face reality. Somewhere in between these two lies the stance you must assume at this point in your life.

Open the Windows

After you have closed the door gently, open the windows. Get some fresh air from a ride in the country, have lunch with a friend, or take a weekend trip. Closing the door does not mean that you have to suffocate or that your life must be stagnant.

Turn the Key

You must close off the hurt and erase the painful past. Feel the healing begin to happen with the security of the past locked behind you. Relish whatever good times you had in the marriage — closeness, children, holidays, parties, etc. But don't turn these into false hopes. Take them for what they were — enjoyable, life-giving moments, similar to the moments yet to come for you.

"Be"

To *be,* in this context, means to let yourself go by relaxing and not worrying. The worst of the storm is ending, even if you do not feel that it is. You are alive. You are safe. Right now you are not supposed to be anywhere else or doing anything else. *Be* whatever *you* want to be. Let the world take care of itself. You take care of you.

Pray

Prayer is not a pious cop-out. It means pleading with God for strength to forgive your former spouse for whatever wrongs may have been done against you and the family. It gives you strength to wish him or her well. And through prayer you thank God for helping you to make it through the tempest of your longest night. You have achieved peaceful silence. This is where your search has been leading you. This is what God has been looking to provide for you, so that he can talk more directly to you and give you a new, resurrected life.

9
Resurrection to a New Life

Death, in Christian theology, is always followed by resurrection. When your marriage died your thoughts were sad, but here are some consoling thoughts about resurrection that should follow as day follows night.

"I died when the judge said, 'Divorce granted!'" But . . .

"I felt resurrection! For the first time in years the sun was finally shining for me. In a certain sense, I felt like Christ coming out of the tomb on Easter Sunday morning. Once more I was in control of my life, the life that the Lord had given me. I could laugh again, and I did. My shouts were cries of relief. 'Hey, world! Hey, everybody! I'm alive! I'm alive!'"

"I died that first night I slept alone." But . . .

"I felt resurrection! My whole life, behind me and ahead of me, danced through my head. Would I find time to call Mary tomorrow, to have lunch with Ann on Thursday, to accept the invitation to take a ride in the country on Sunday? In a matter of moments, I felt like a child expectantly awaiting Santa Claus on Christmas Eve. I felt reborn. I felt resurrection!"

"I died the day I sold my house." But . . .

"I felt resurrection! What was dust anymore? Or leaky basements? Or uncut grass? Where I live now is heaven. I've made myself comfortable. Friends come to visit. My heart is my home. That's my address now. During the last troubled years of my marriage I never really felt I was home. Now I welcome the whole world into my heart — into my home."

"I died the day my spouse remarried." But . . .

"I felt resurrection! If the door between us was ever open, now it was closed. Let someone else do the worrying. I had told myself over and over that there was no way I could endure this ultimate hurt. But now I have more than endured it. Here I am going stronger than ever and liking it. I have said a prayer for both of them. I have entrusted them to the Lord."

"I died when my child went out on his own." But . . .

"I felt resurrection! For I had done everything possible to prepare him for adulthood. I felt proud of how well I had done my job. Now I no longer bother to notice the scars that used to worry me so. All I can see is a grown-up person ready to face the world. Alleluia!"

From Death to Resurrection

Although a marriage can die, the two people who were married can be resurrected. The mystery of all of nature is death and rebirth. This same mystery is present in the human experience. This is how God made the universe and how God made you.

When trouble brewed in your marriage you no doubt were tempted to blame God. Why did he set you up for a divorce? Why did he ever bring you together? Why do you have to suffer so?

But God is not at fault. His love is ever present and his grace will never fail you. The fault lies with the human love that is not functioning as it should. God always works within the human condition. He gives you your freedom. He supports and sustains you. He does not overrule your choices, your humanness, and your failures. God desires what is good for you, but he always allows you to be you. When you blame God for your suffering you are projecting your own anger and bitterness on to him. God becomes the scapegoat. Your gift of faith gives you the opportunity to understand your own human frailty and weakness and also God's power to heal you and to raise you up.

"I had no idea how I was going to make it through Christmas. My ten children and myself were on welfare. I was ashamed to tell anybody about our plight. Since I did not have enough money even for food I couldn't think about buying presents. But on Christmas Eve one of the kids found a $1,000.00 cashier's check in the mailbox. It was from 'a friend.' Ever since then my belief in God has been restored."

When everyone else stops caring, God continues to care. That is why God is God. Especially at this time in your life you need somebody close to you — somebody who knows you intimately, who truly cares about you, and who understands what you are going through. God is that Somebody.

The crisis of a divorce has a way of bringing you back to the basics of life. In Chinese the word "crisis" denotes both danger and *opportunity*. God is that opportunity in your life. Ever-present, he is intermingled in the roots of your life. And this crisis has served to make God more clearly visible to you.

New Relationships

Many of the elements not present in your relationship with your former spouse can now be present in your relationship with God:

Availability. God always has time for you and he is never far away. As the saying goes, "When God seems far away, *who moved?*"

Support. God accepts you as you are. He made you, and he supports you as you are. He does not try to change you to be something that you are not. The only change that he asks of you is that you bloom in his goodness.

Dialogue. When you speak with God he will answer you — not always in the way you want. But he will answer, nevertheless.

Love. That love has gone awry in your marriage is not the fault of God. His love for you is without end. And the more love you give him the more you will receive in return.

Easter Resurrection

On the first day of the week, at dawn, the women came to the tomb bringing the spices they had prepared. They found the stone rolled back from the tomb; but when they entered the tomb, they did not find the body of the Lord Jesus. While they were still at a loss over what to think of this, two men in dazzling garments stood beside them. Terrified, the women bowed to the ground. The men said to them: "Why do you search for the Living One among the dead? He is not here; he has been raised up. Remember what he said to you while he was still in Galilee — that the Son of Man must be delivered into the hands of sinful men, and be crucified, and on the third day rise again." With this reminder, his words came back to them.

On their return from the tomb, they told all these things to the Eleven and the others. The women were Mary of Magdala, Joanna, and Mary the mother of James. The other women with them also told the apostles, but the story seemed like nonsense and they refused to believe them. Peter, however, got up and ran to the tomb. He stooped down but could see nothing but the wrappings. So he went away full of amazement at what had occurred (Luke 24:1-12).

This Gospel story tells us that the suffering and dying Christ has risen from the dead. He has conquered the sin of the world. Death has been completely overshadowed by Resurrection. The One that they all saw die a horrible death is now more alive and well than ever.

The Resurrection of Jesus was not the only miracle that took place on Easter morning. The women and the apostles who also "died" with Christ were resurrected when he came out of the tomb. Previously, Peter had denied and Thomas had doubted. Every one of the apostles but John had run away. But once they saw with their own eyes that the dead Christ was no longer in the tomb, they themselves rose from their despair, doubt, and depression.

The Resurrection is a great mystery and a challenge — the dead Christ coming back to life, his dead followers also being reborn and coming back to life.

The ultimate mystery of your divorce is that through Christ and his tremendous power, *you are alive* and *resurrected*. "Why do you search for the Living One among the dead? He is not here; he has been raised up" (Luke 24:5-6).

For more information about the Beginning Experience please write to:

> The Beginning Experience
> Central Office
> 3100 W. 41st Street
> Sioux Falls, South Dakota 57105